W9-BOD-984

WITHDRAWN

SOCCER
How It Works

Sports Illustrated KIDS

BY SUZANNE BAZEMORE

Consultant:
Meade Brooks
Physics Professor
Collin College
Fresco, Texas

CAPSTONE PRESS
a capstone imprint

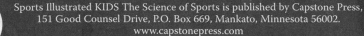

092009
005620LKS10

 Books published by Capstone Press are manufactured with paper
containing at least 10 percent post-consumer waste.

Library of Congress Cataloging-in-Publication Data
Bazemore, Suzanne.
    Soccer: how it works / by Suzanne Bazemore.
    p. cm. — (Sports Illustrated KIDS. The science of sports)
    Includes bibliographical references and index.
    Summary: "Describes the science behind the sport of soccer, including kicking,
ball control, and goalkeeping" — Provided by publisher.
    ISBN 978-1-4296-4025-1 (library binding)
    ISBN 978-1-4296-4876-9 (paperback)
1. Soccer — Juvenile literature. I. Title. II. Series.
GV943.25.B39 2010
796.334 — dc22   2009043261

Editorial Credits
Anthony Wacholtz, editor; Ted Williams, designer; Jo Miller, media researcher;
    Eric Manske, production specialist

Design Elements
Shutterstock/Eray Haciosmanoglu; kamphi

Photo Credits
El Universal via Getty Images Inc./Marco Antonio Valdez, 40–41 (bottom)
Getty Images Inc./AFP/Alexa Reyes, 25 (all); AFP/Ben Stansall, 44; AFP/Frank Perry, 42;
    AFP/Oliver Lang, 43; AFP/Patrick Hertzog, 14 (right); Bob Thomas, 16;
    LatinContent/Jamie Pavon, 23 (bottom); Phil Cole, 45
MLS via Getty Images Inc./Scott Priby, 32
Real Madrid via Getty Images Inc./Angel Martinez, 38
Shutterstock/Photosani, cover (field); Ronald Sumners, cover (soccer ball);
    Worldpics, cover (net); Xtremer, cover (grass)
Sports Illustrated/Al Tielemans, 12, 31; Bob Martin, 7, 14 (left), 15 (both), 20, 21 (top), 22,
    26, 34, 41 (top right); Bob Rosato, cover (top); David E. Klutho, 18–19; Simon Bruty, cover
    (bottom left, middle, and bottom right), 1, 3, 4–5, 6, 8, 9, 10, 11, 13, 17, 19 (right), 21 (bottom),
    23 (top), 24 (both), 27, 28–29 (inset), 30, 33 (both), 35, 36, 37, 39

TABLE OF CONTENTS

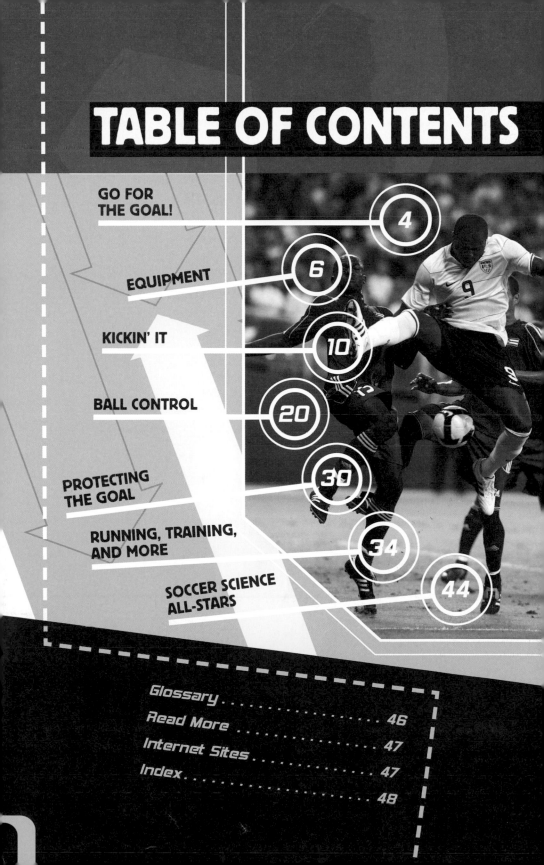

"Goal!" yells the announcer after an amazing bicycle kick. With great goals and thrilling saves, soccer is one of the world's most popular sports. The Fédération Internationale de Football Association (FIFA) is soccer's international governing body. The association ranks teams from more than 200 countries and territories.

Soccer players are highly skilled at dribbling, heading, and shooting the ball. Whatever the skill, science unravels the mystery behind the game. All you need is a little knowledge and a lot of practice. Maybe one day you will bend it like David Beckham, dribble through opponents like Ronaldo, or score like Mia Hamm. But first you need a ball, a field, and a lesson in science.

inertia
Once the ball is kicked, it will stay in motion until outside forces, such as friction or the goalkeeper's block, act on it.

friction
A player's shoes create friction against the turf or grass, helping the player run.

4

reaction time
The goalkeeper must have quick reflexes to stop the ball from going into the net.

CHAPTER 1

CORE OF THE GAME – THE BALL

Technology has helped make soccer balls more durable. Current soccer balls are covered with synthetic leather. They hold their shape better than the real leather balls used in the past.

Most soccer balls have 32 panels and up to 2,000 stitches. The seams in the ball reduce **DRAG**, making the ball's movement easier to predict.

Air is pumped through a small hole, called a valve, into a rubber bladder. When air is forced into the ball, the air inside the ball becomes more tightly packed than the air outside the ball. The pressure of the air molecules colliding inside the ball make it firm. The firmness of the ball makes it bounce better.

DRAG — backward force on an object because of air resistance

The energy of a kick is temporarily stored by the compressed air molecules in the ball. The ball springs off the player's foot as the air molecules release the **POTENTIAL ENERGY**. Balls that are overinflated tend to bounce off a player's foot with more energy. Overinflated balls also put more force back on the foot. The extra force could cause an injury. Balls that are underinflated may feel softer and more comfortable when kicked. However, underinflated balls often won't bounce as much or travel as far as a properly inflated ball.

POTENTIAL ENERGY — the stored energy of an object

LACE UP

Cleats or turf shoes? The best shoes to wear depend on the type of field and the field conditions. Many factors affect the condition of the pitch, or soccer field.

Turf shoes have many short studs on the bottom of the shoe. But since the studs are short, they can't dig into soft ground. They work well on hard, dry ground because they distribute the impact of running more evenly across the foot.

On soft, wet ground, cleats dig into the grass. The cleats give runners traction. Traction occurs from friction between the soccer player's shoes and the field. Molded cleats provide enough traction for most conditions. Special soft ground shoes are made for deep turf or muddy conditions.

cleats

Players choose shoes based on how much **FRICTION** is needed. As a player runs one direction, the shoes produce friction in the opposite direction. The rougher the surfaces, the more friction they produce.

FRICTION — the force caused by rubbing one object against another

Although a kick seems simple, there is a lot of science behind it. The law of conservation of energy states that energy is neither created or destroyed. Soccer players transfer energy from their feet or heads to the ball. Isaac Newton, an English scientist, created three laws of motion. These laws explain how energy is transferred to a soccer ball.

Newton's first law, the law of **INERTIA**, states that an object at rest will stay at rest unless an outside force is applied to it. Similarly, an object in motion will stay in motion unless another force acts on it. So a ball won't move until you kick it. Once the ball is kicked, it tends to stay in motion unless a force, such as friction or another player, stops it.

Newton's second law involves force, mass, and **ACCELERATION**. Force and acceleration have magnitude, or size, and direction. For example, a player's foot applies a certain amount of force on the ball in one direction. Friction applies force in the opposite direction.

Objects with more mass have more inertia. They tend to strongly resist changing their motion. The acceleration of an object depends on the force that is acting on it. For example, the harder the ball is kicked, the faster it will go. The ball will eventually be slowed by drag in the air and friction on the ground.

ACCELERATION — the change in speed of a moving body
INERTIA — an object's state in which the object stays at rest or keeps moving in the same direction until a force acts on the object

Newton's third law states that for every action, there is an equal and opposite reaction. If a player's foot applies force to the ball, the ball applies force to the player's foot too.

Muscles provide the power for the kick. Energy transfers down parts of the body that are connected by the hip and knee joints. Joints serve as pivot points for the bones to turn around. The long bones act as levers that help the foot launch the ball.

For hard shots, players point their toes forward and kick with the upper part of their foot near the laces. The foot transfers energy to the ball because of its **VELOCITY**. The transfer happens when the foot spins around the knee and hits the ball.

VELOCITY — a measurement of both the speed and direction an object is moving

Ball speed during the kick can be 59 to 115 feet (18 to 35 meters) per second. Ball speed can be increased with good technique. One way to increase ball speed is to change the **ANGULAR VELOCITY** of the lower leg. The angular velocity measures how fast the lower leg pivots around the knee. A higher foot velocity will increase the velocity of the ball.

Other factors also affect the ball's velocity:

▶ PREFERRED FOOT — Are you right-footed or left-footed? Players kick harder with their best foot. The harder a ball is kicked, the higher its velocity.

▶ TYPE OF KICK — Powerful kicks are faster. But speed isn't everything — it's important to hit the target. It may be worth making a less powerful kick if it's more accurate.

ANGULAR VELOCITY — the rate of change of an object's angle as it moves around a central point

When it comes to kicking, the body acts like several simple machines. Joints are the pivots, and bones are the levers. Muscles apply force to the bones to move them around the joints. Muscles store energy so they can apply a lot of force and produce a powerful kick.

THE BICYCLE KICK

Pelé perfected the bicycle kick. This rare kick demonstrates the conservation of angular momentum. Pelé pushed off the ground, spun, and kicked the ball while he was horizontal. He transferred his angular velocity to the ball as his body spun in the air. This kick is useful when the player wants to move the ball in the direction opposite to where he or she is facing.

Here's how kicking works:

1. The upper leg muscles pull the lower leg forward.
2. **CENTRIPETAL FORCE** accelerates the lower leg around the knee, which serves as a pivot.
3. The lower leg whips forward and makes the foot move three times faster than the leg at the knee.
4. As the knee bends, angular velocity transfers **KINETIC ENERGY** from the thigh to the lower leg and foot.

CENTRIPETAL FORCE — the force that makes an object rotating in a circle follow a curved path
KINETIC ENERGY — the energy of a moving object

FOLLOW THE BALL'S PATH

According to Newton's first law of motion, a ball kicked in the center will go straight. However, striking across the ball creates spin. The ball will curve in the direction of the spin. This curving, or bending, is caused by the Magnus effect. This effect happens when air molecules apply sideways forces to the ball. These forces are caused by uneven air spinning around the ball.

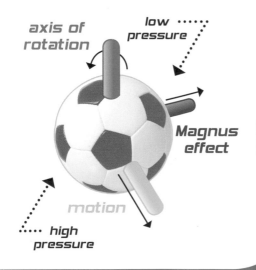

axis of rotation

low pressure

Magnus effect

motion

high pressure

The Magnus effect was named after German physicist Heinrich Gustav Magnus. Magnus studied the effects of a ball moving through fluids in the 1800s.

A bent ball's velocity is slower than a ball kicked in the center. But a bent ball can get around a wall of defensive players during a free kick. David Beckham and other pros can bend the path of the ball. In 1997, Roberto Carlos showed his ability to bend the ball's path during a game between Brazil and France. In fact, he bent it so much that a ball boy to the far right of the net ducked because he thought he would be hit.

BECKHAM'S BEND

Researchers studied how to score goals by bending the ball's path like David Beckham does. They found that he kicks the ball 80 miles (129 kilometers) per hour with the instep of his right foot. He hits the ball 3 inches (8 centimeters) to the right of the ball's center. This off-center kick puts a spin on the ball. The spin creates Magnus forces that cause the ball to bend to the left. As the ball approaches the crossbar, it slows to 40 miles (64 kilometers) per hour. Then it drops into the upper left corner of the net.

SPINNING SCIENCE

Because of Newton's laws of motion, a soccer ball will move in the direction of the forces applied to it. Many forces act on the ball once it is kicked. Force from the kick is in one direction. Friction is in the opposite direction. Forces applied in opposite directions tend to cancel each other out. The stronger force cancels the weaker force, and the ball will move in the direction of the stronger force.

Air molecules also apply force to the ball. Drag from the air opposes the thrust of the kick, and lift opposes gravity. Bernoulli's principle explains how pressure differences in the air provide lift to airplane wings so they can fly. Fluids that move quickly, such as air, apply less pressure than fluids that move slowly. Air moves faster over the top of an airplane wing, which is curved, than beneath it. Since there is less air pressure above the wing than below it, the wing lifts. As speed increases, so does lift. For the airplane to fly, lift must be stronger than the force of gravity.

Bernoulli's principle

low pressure

high pressure

air movement

These forces and pressure differences also affect a spinning soccer ball and produce the Magnus effect. The air in front of the ball is under higher pressure and moves slower. The air behind the ball is under lower pressure and moves faster. The Bernoulli effect causes the ball to spin toward the lower pressure. The fast, spinning ball creates air turbulence that reduces drag. But when the ball slows down at the end of its path, the airflow becomes smooth and drag increases. This drag can cause the ball to drop into the goal.

CHAPTER 3

▷BALL CONTROL

Good technique isn't only about kicking. Understanding the science behind headers, traps, throw-ins, and passing can lead to better ball control.

HEADING THE BALL

Newton's third law of motion comes into play when a player heads the ball. During a header, the speed of a player's head determines the speed of the ball. **MOMENTUM** transfers from the head to the ball. The neck muscles can move the head a few inches, transferring even more momentum to the ball.

MOMENTUM — a property of a moving object equal to its mass times its velocity

momentum = mass x velocity

mass

velocity ⊙

momentum ⊙

A glancing header redirects the ball either for a pass or to make a shot on goal. A diving header applies force to the ball because of the speed of the striker's body.

TRAP FACTOR

The purpose of trapping the ball is different from most other soccer skills. Instead of applying force or transferring momentum, the player wants to stop the ball. To get the ball to stop, the player's foot absorbs the ball's momentum. The foot moves back with the ball on impact until the ball stops.

The key to trapping is to keep the body loose to absorb the ball's momentum. When trapping, players want to keep the ball as close as possible. They don't want to send it in the other direction toward an opponent.

When the ball arrives at a steep angle, the player contains the bounce by placing a foot or knee over the ball. This trap requires good timing. The player can also use the instep of his or her foot to cushion the ball and absorb the momentum. The ball should land at the player's feet.

Chest traps work the same way as a foot trap. The player uses his or her body to cushion the ball and absorb the ball's momentum.

THROW IT IN!

Throw-ins help a team set up offensive plays. They can also create scoring opportunities. All throw-ins must come from behind the head. Following that rule puts science on the thrower's side. It allows the thrower's arms to act as levers for the ball as they rotate around the shoulders and elbows. The throwing motion gives the ball more velocity.

▶ SHORT THROWS

During a short throw, a player releases the ball at a 45-degree angle to a nearby teammate. The teammate can take the ball or pass it back to the thrower, who might have a better view of the field. This give-and-go technique also works for dribbling.

▶ LONG THROWS

For a long throw, a player throws the ball from the edge of the field into the goal area. The ball starts closer to the goal, giving the team with the possession an advantage. Also, the offsides rule doesn't apply to throw-ins.

Running allows the thrower to transfer additional momentum to the ball. The thrower accelerates during the run. This acceleration increases the force applied to the ball. Then the body whips forward, transferring angular velocity from the arms to the hands, and then finally to the ball. Whether a throw-in is long or short, the player should follow through. Following through maximizes the force applied to the ball.

FLIP THROWS

The flip throw is rarely used because it is extremely difficult. This throw uses a front handspring to apply force over a long distance. Force on the ball begins when the athlete is upside down during the handstand and the ball is on the ground. The player applies force to the ball during the flip. The ball is then released overhead and catapulted a long distance.

THE IMPORTANCE OF PASSING

For accurate passes, players kick the ball with the insides of their feet. Kicking with the instep gives the player more control over the ball because of the high surface area. In these types of passes, the leg acts like a golf putter. The main focus is to be accurate, not powerful.

The toe has the least surface area and the player has little ball control. That's why soccer players often use the insides of their feet to pass the ball.

Scientists have found that tired players don't pass accurately. Tired athletes were 62 percent less accurate with passes than they were at the beginning of the game.

Long passes are similar to power shots because the ball is kicked with the top of the foot. The top of the foot has less surface area than the inside of the foot, so accuracy is more difficult. But because of the natural motion of the leg swinging around the hip and knee joints, greater force is applied to the ball. This power is greater than that of the side-to-side movement of the leg during a regular pass.

Teams on offense need to create space to make the opposing defense run more. Players create space by spreading out and passing the ball using patterns and drills learned in practice.

Players take a running start during a corner kick to create more force on the ball. This long pass puts the ball near the goal for the kicker's teammates.

When passing the ball, a player tries to predict the speed of the teammate receiving the ball. The passing player kicks the ball at an angle so that the ball will arrive where the runner is going.

PASS PLAYS

There are several ways that players can open up the field by passing.

• **Cross the Ball**

Create a scoring opportunity by passing the ball to the space in front of the goal.

• **Give and Go**

Pass the ball to a teammate. Run behind the defender to an open space. Your teammate can pass it back to you or another open player.

• **Third Attacker**

Pass the ball to a teammate, who will pass it to another teammate.

CHAPTER 4

▷ PROTECTING THE GOAL

Goalkeepers are the only players allowed to use their hands. They can perform traps and throws no other players can do. But a goalkeeper still has to trap the ball correctly, or the other team might score. When throwing the ball, a goalkeeper needs to get it to a teammate or clear it from around the goal.

▶ THE CATCH

A goalkeeper catches the ball by trapping it with the hands and pulling it into the body. The body absorbs most of the ball's momentum.

▶ THE DIVE

Diving for the ball can lead to an impressive save. Goalkeepers cut off the angle of the striker. As the keeper moves closer to the striker, the striker has fewer angles to get the ball into the net. The keeper moves forward and dives to the ball after the kick. The forward momentum of the goalkeeper changes the ball's direction after he makes contact with it. A keeper moving backward might accidentally allow a goal by not redirecting the ball.

WATCH THE HIPS

Eighty percent of penalty kicks result in a score. The velocity of the ball is often too fast for the goalkeeper's reaction time. The goalkeeper looks at the striker's hips to predict the direction of the kick. If a right-footed striker's hips are squarely facing the goal, the ball will go to the right of the goalkeeper. If the striker's hips are angled away from the goalkeeper, the ball will go to the goalkeeper's left.

▶ THE PUNCH

A goalkeeper might not be able to reach the ball to catch it, or the box might be too crowded. In those situations, he or she can punch the ball away from the goal. A one-handed punch deflects the ball, but it may continue in the direction of the goal. If the ball needs to go the opposite direction, the keeper uses both hands. Punching puts Newton's first law of motion into action. That ball won't stop heading toward the goal by itself. Force must be applied for it to go the other direction.

To punch, the player makes a fist with the thumb out of the way but not tucked in. The fingers make a flat surface.

Punching is used to get the ball away from the goal, not to redirect it around the frame.

▶ THE PARRY

Parrying the ball is a technique that the goalkeeper uses to tip the ball over the net. The goalkeeper uses this technique if the ball is out of reach to catch. Fingertips or the palm of the hand can be used, but the hand must face forward. The purpose of a parry is to deflect the ball off the fingertips and redirect its momentum.

▶ THE THROW

Sometimes goalkeepers roll or throw the ball to their teammates instead of kicking it. Goalkeepers run with the ball for about 6 feet (1.8 meters). This long contact with the ball gives the ball more momentum. The momentum of the ball helps it travel a long distance. The goalkeeper can aim the ball better with a throw than with a kick.

CHAPTER 5

▷ RUNNING, TRAINING, AND MORE

READY TO RUN

Soccer players can become better runners by working on their technique. Dr. Michael Yessis, a scientist who studies athletes, says that there are three phases of running: push-off, flight, and support.

1. Push-off gets the player off the ground and creates horizontal force for speed.

2. When in flight, the runner targets the best stride length. The best stride length allows the feet to plant under the **CENTER OF GRAVITY**.

3. During the support phase, leg muscles hold up the body and prepare for another push-off. Players should avoid up-and-down movements that waste energy, such as head-bobbing.

CENTER OF GRAVITY — the point on an object at which it can balance

Improvement in any of these phases can increase a player's speed. According to Dr. Yessis, world-class sprinters move their bodies just 1 inch (2.5 centimeters) off center while running. Bouncing an extra .25 inch (.6 centimeter) with each step during a game wastes as much energy as climbing five flights of stairs.

RUNNING THE DISTANCE

A player runs about 5 to 8 miles (8 to 13 kilometers) during a game. The initial acceleration occurs when two things happen. First, the runner's stride length increases and the legs move farther apart. Second, the runner's number of steps increases as the legs move more quickly. After about 100 feet (30 meters), the runner reaches top speed. That's when the ability to keep up the speed — called secondary acceleration — becomes important.

AEROBIC AND ANAEROBIC EXERCISE

Muscles make two types of energy. Aerobic energy is made with oxygen, and anaerobic energy is made without oxygen. The body makes energy in stages. The first stage doesn't need oxygen. But if oxygen is available, aerobic energy is created.

The oxygen used to make aerobic energy comes from the air you breathe. Blood passes through the lungs and carries oxygen to the muscle cells. Muscles use oxygen to burn glucose, a type of sugar in the body that is used for energy.

As the body demands more oxygen, the player breathes harder. Sometimes the body uses energy faster than the lungs can supply oxygen. That's when the muscles make anaerobic energy.

Children's and adults' bodies work differently. Children's bodies use mostly aerobic energy. The body gets better at making anaerobic energy over time. Since younger soccer players don't use as much anaerobic energy as adults, they usually play shorter games. They also play on smaller fields and use more player substitutions.

Soccer players use both aerobic and anaerobic energy. Midfielders have a high aerobic ability. They develop the endurance to move forward and backward as they attack and defend. Central defenders and goalkeepers don't need as much aerobic ability as a midfielder. Fullbacks and strikers are somewhere in between.

TO THE WEIGHT ROOM

Muscles get power for running and kicking by burning glucose. Soccer players go to the weight room often to get their muscles into shape. They use an elliptical or run on a treadmill to build endurance. They lift weights to increase their muscle strength.

Soreness results from muscle damage. When the body performs exercise at a level it's not used to, the muscle fibers tear. The body's immune system tries to stop the damage by sending in cells and proteins. However, these rescue attempts cause pain and swelling. The soreness, called delayed onset muscle soreness (DOMS), usually isn't felt for a day or two. The soreness can last up to a week.

The good news is that muscles recover. Proper weight training helps players' muscles get used to the tough exercise during a soccer match. Stretching can help prevent DOMS.

TRAINING FOR THE GAME

Athletes train their muscles for speed and agility using plyometric training, which involves high-intensity exercises. For example, jumping in practice prepares the player for jumping to head the ball during a game.

Soccer players need strength to run and stop quickly. Stopping suddenly and changing direction to get around an opponent is called cutting. To cut, the player plants one foot in front, opposite the cutting direction. When the knee bends, the thigh muscles stretch and provide power to shove off the ground.

Many training programs exist. FIFA developed its own training program called "The 11." This warm-up routine provides 11 exercises that focus on stability, weight training, and plyometric training.

Soccer games are intense. Players run hard every 30 seconds and sprint at top speed every 90 seconds. They dribble the ball only 2 percent of the time. Many plays involve just one touch on the ball. Much of a player's time is spent covering the opponent or helping a teammate.

The types of movement a player does most depend on the player's position. The closer an exercise is to a movement in the sport, the better trained that muscle will be. Strikers have the most intense activity and quick movements. Defenders spend more time moving backward. Strikers and defenders benefit from speed and agility training. Midfielders perform fewer turns and benefit from long-distance running.

FUEL FOR THE GAME

Soccer players need fuel. The body uses one-third to one-half of its stored energy during a game. A high-carbohydrate meal eaten three to four hours before a game gives players enough energy to play.

Players can eat lean proteins, but they should avoid foods high in fat. Fatty foods take too long to digest, and players need empty stomachs during the game. The heart pumps blood to the stomach to aid digestion. But when the player starts running, the muscles also need blood. If the stomach is still trying to digest food, the player could suffer from cramps.

Players should eat a balanced diet. Vitamins and minerals are important, too. Iron, for example, helps carry oxygen in the blood. Players who are too nervous to eat should drink a carbohydrate drink 30 minutes to an hour before the game. They should also drink plenty of water to stay hydrated during the game.

Dehydrated players who have lost 5 percent of their body weight lose 30 percent of their work ability.

CARB DRINKS VS. MILK

Researchers discovered that 2-percent chocolate milk is as good as or better than carbohydrate drinks at restoring glucose. For the experiment, people rode a bike for an hour, rested for four hours, then rode again. When they rode the second time, there was a difference in the group members' performance. The group that drank 1 pint (.5 liter) of 2-percent chocolate milk performed 43 to 51 percent better than the group that drank carb drinks. Why? Scientists think it is because of the extra proteins and fats.

CHAPTER 6

▷SOCCER SCIENCE ALL-STARS

Now you understand the science behind playing and training for soccer. See how these athletes put science to the test.

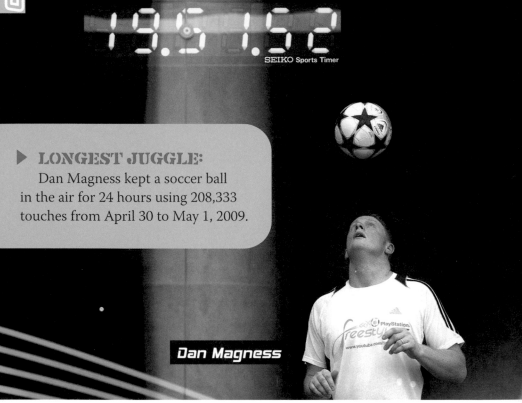

SEIKO Sports Timer

▶ **LONGEST JUGGLE:**
Dan Magness kept a soccer ball in the air for 24 hours using 208,333 touches from April 30 to May 1, 2009.

Dan Magness

▶ **MOST JUGGLES IN ONE MINUTE:**
Chloe Hegland kept the ball in the air for one minute using 339 touches on November 3, 2007.

▶ **LONGEST TIME HEADING THE BALL:**
Thomas Lundman headed the ball for 8 hours, 32 minutes, and 3 seconds on February 27, 2004.

▶ **FASTEST WORLD CUP GOAL AFTER KICKOFF:**
In 2002, Turkish soccer player Hakan Sükür scored against Korea Republic 11 seconds into the match.

▶ **MOST OVERALL GOALS IN WORLD CUPS:**
Ronaldo scored 15 goals for Brazil from 1998 to 2006.

People around the world, whether they are young or old, enjoy the art in motion that is soccer. You have an edge because you know the science behind the moves. All you need now is a ball and a field!

45

GLOSSARY

acceleration (ak-sel-uh-RAY-shuhn) — the change in speed of a moving body

angular velocity (ANG-yoo-luhr vuh-LOSS-uh-tee) — the rate of change of an object's angle as it moves around a central point

center of gravity (SEN-tur UHV GRAV-uh-tee) — the point on an object at which it can balance

centripetal force (sen-TRI-puh-tuhl FORS) — the force that makes an object rotating in a circle follow a curved path

drag (DRAG) — air resistance on an object moving through air

friction (FRIK-shuhn) — the force caused by rubbing one object against another

inertia (in-UR-shuh) — an object's state in which the object stays at rest or keeps moving in the same direction until a force acts on the object

kinetic energy (ki-NET-ik EN-ur-jee) — the energy of a moving object

lift (LIFT) — the upward force created by a solid moving through a gas or liquid

momentum (moh-MEN-tuhm) — a property of a moving object equal to its mass times its velocity

potential energy (puh-TEN-shuhl EN-ur-jee) — the stored energy of an object

velocity (vuh-LOSS-uh-tee) — a measurement of both the speed and direction an object is moving

READ MORE

Beckham, David. *David Beckham's Soccer Skills.* New York: Collins, 2006.

Crisfield, Deborah. *The Everything Kids' Soccer Book: Rules, Techniques, and More About Your Favorite Sport!* 2nd ed. Everything Kids. Avon, Mass.: Adams Media Corp., 2009.

Solway, Andrew. *Sports Science.* Why Science Matters. Chicago: Heinemann, 2009.

Thomas, Keltie. *How Soccer Works.* How Sports Work. Toronto, Ontario, Canada: Maple Tree Press, 2007.

INTERNET SITES

FactHound offers a safe, fun way to find Internet sites related to this book. All of the sites on Facthound have been researched by our staff.

Here's all you do:

Visit *www.facthound.com*

FactHound will fetch the best sites for you!

INDEX